On the Farm

by Sascha Goddard

OXFORD
UNIVERSITY PRESS
AUSTRALIA & NEW ZEALAND

Mum and Dad get up.

The sun is up.

ram

A ram runs to the pen.

A carrot is in the mud.

carrot

Mum digs it up.

egg

Dad picks up the egg.

The duck is in the muck.

The duck pecks.

Mum and Dad on the deck. It is sunset.

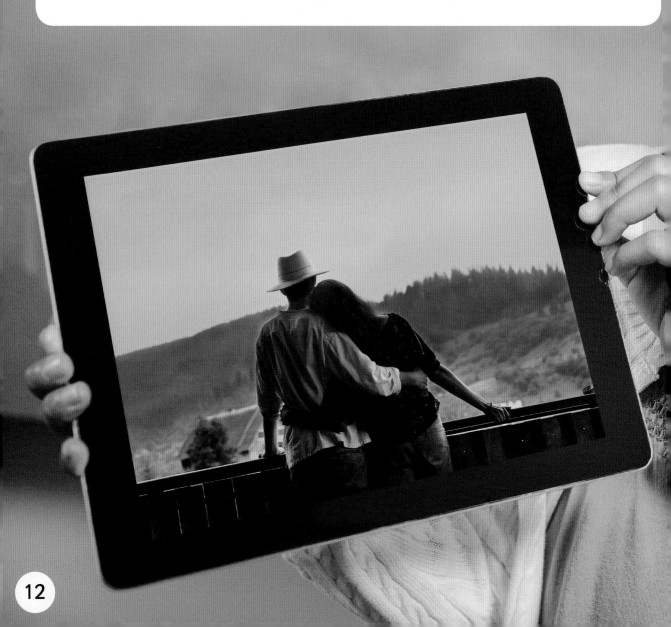